contents

NZ, Canada, US and UK readers
Please note that Australian cup and spoon
measurements are metric. A quick conversion
guide appears on page 63.

chicken and broccoli with oyster sauce

½ cup (125ml) chicken stock
¼ cup (60ml) oyster sauce
2 teaspoons cornflour
2 teaspoons caster sugar
½ teaspoon sesame oil
1 tablespoon vegetable oil
500g chicken breast fillets, sliced thinly
4 green onions, chopped
1 tablespoon bottled grated ginger
2 teaspoons bottled crushed garlic
500g broccoli florets
2 tablespoons water

Whisk stock, sauce, cornflour, sugar and sesame oil in small bowl until well combined.
Heat half of the vegetable oil in wok or large frying pan; stir-fry chicken, in batches, until just cooked through.
Heat remaining vegetable oil in same wok; stir-fry onion, ginger, garlic, broccoli and the water until broccoli is tender. Return chicken to wok with sauce mixture; stir-fry until chicken is hot and sauce boils and thickens slightly.

serves 4
per serving 12.8g fat; 1194kJ (285 cal)
on the table in 20 minutes

linguine with tuna, lemon and rocket

425g can tuna in oil
500g linguine pasta
2 tablespoons extra virgin olive oil
2 teaspoons bottled crushed garlic
2 medium dried red chillies, sliced thinly
1/3 cup (80ml) lemon juice
100g baby rocket

Drain tuna over small bowl and reserve oil.
You will need 1/3 cup (80ml) oil.
Cook pasta in large saucepan of boiling water,
uncovered, until just tender; drain, return to pan.
Meanwhile, heat tuna oil and olive oil gently in
large non-stick frying pan, add garlic and chilli;
cook, stirring, until fragrant.
Add tuna and break into chunks. Remove
from heat, then add juice.
Add tuna mixture to hot pasta with rocket;
toss gently to combine.

serves 4
per serving 35.7g fat; 3442kJ (822 cal)
on the table in 15 minutes

beef with mushroom and red wine sauce

1 tablespoon olive oil
4 beef rib-eye steaks (800g)
30g butter
8 spring onions (200g), quartered
1 teaspoon bottled crushed garlic
1 cup (250ml) dry red wine
1/2 cup (125ml) beef stock
6 flat mushrooms, quartered
2 tablespoons chopped fresh flat-leaf parsley

Heat oil in large frying pan. Cook beef until browned on both sides and cooked as desired; remove from pan.
Add butter and onion to same pan; cook, stirring, until onion is browned lightly.
Stir in garlic, wine and stock; bring to a boil. Reduce heat; simmer, covered, 10 minutes.
Add mushrooms; cook, stirring, until mushrooms are soft. Stir in parsley.
Serve beef with mushroom and red wine sauce and, if desired, kumara mash.

serves 4
per serving 23.3g fat; 1813kJ (433 cal)
on the table in 40 minutes

mushroom pizza

We used packaged pizza bases measuring 15cm
across for this recipe, but any fresh or frozen variety
would also be suitable. Pizza cheese is a commercial
blend of mozzarella, parmesan and cheddar.

4 x 112g pizza bases
1½ cups (185g) grated pizza cheese
150g flat mushrooms, sliced thinly
100g fetta cheese, crumbled
2 tablespoons chopped fresh chives

Preheat oven to hot.
Place pizza bases on oven tray. Sprinkle half
of the pizza cheese over bases.
Divide mushrooms, fetta cheese and chives
among bases. Top with remaining pizza cheese.
Bake, uncovered, in hot oven 15 minutes or until
pizza tops are browned lightly and bases are crisp.

serves 4
per serving 20.3g fat; 2266kJ (541 cal)
on the table in 25 minutes

chilli and honey beef

4 boneless beef sirloin steaks (800g)
2 tablespoons lime juice
1 tablespoon olive oil
2 tablespoons honey
1 teaspoon dried chilli flakes
1 teaspoon bottled crushed garlic

Combine ingredients in large bowl; stand, covered, 10 minutes.
Cook beef on heated oiled grill plate (or grill or barbecue) until cooked as desired.
Serve beef with steamed green vegetables, if desired.

serves 4
per serving 17.1g fat; 1526kJ (365 cal)
on the table in 25 minutes

zucchini and mushroom omelette

10g butter
1 teaspoon bottled crushed garlic
25g button mushrooms, sliced thinly
$^1/_4$ cup (50g) grated zucchini
1 green onion, chopped finely
2 eggs
1 tablespoon water
$^1/_4$ cup (30g) grated cheddar cheese

Heat half of the butter in small non-stick
frying pan, add garlic and mushrooms; cook,
stirring, until mushrooms are just browned.
Add zucchini and onion; cook, stirring, until
zucchini begins to soften. Remove vegetable
mixture from pan; cover to keep warm.
Whisk eggs and the water together in small bowl,
add cheese; whisk until combined.
Heat remaining butter in same pan, pour
egg mixture into pan; cook, tilting pan,
over medium heat until almost set.
Place vegetable mixture evenly over half of
the omelette; using eggslice, flip other half over
vegetable mixture. Using eggslice, slide omelette
gently onto serving plate.

serves 1
per serving 29.2g fat; 1506kJ (360 cal)
on the table in 20 minutes

spicy orange lamb noodle stir-fry

750g lamb strips
1 teaspoon sesame oil
1 tablespoon finely grated orange rind
2 teaspoons bottled crushed garlic
1 teaspoon bottled grated ginger
$1/2$ cup (125ml) light soy sauce
1 tablespoon black bean sauce
1 tablespoon brown sugar
250g dried wheat noodles
2 tablespoons peanut oil
200g snow peas, sliced thinly lengthways
1 medium fresh red chilli, seeded, sliced
$1/4$ cup (60ml) beef stock

Combine lamb with sesame oil, rind, garlic, ginger, sauces and sugar in large bowl.
Cook noodles in large saucepan of boiling water, uncovered, until just tender; drain.
Heat a little of the peanut oil in wok or large frying pan; add snow peas, stir-fry until tender, remove from wok.
Drain lamb from marinade, reserve marinade. Heat a little more of the peanut oil in wok; stir-fry lamb, in batches, until browned and cooked through.
Return snow peas, lamb and reserved marinade to wok with chilli and stock; bring to a boil. Add noodles; stir-fry until heated through.

serves 4
per serving 18g fat; 2365kJ (565 cal)
on the table in 25 minutes

coriander and chilli grilled chicken

6 chicken thigh fillets (660g), halved
coriander chilli sauce
8 green onions, chopped coarsely
2 teaspoons bottled crushed garlic
1 teaspoon bottled chopped red chilli
1/4 cup loosely packed fresh coriander
1 teaspoon sugar
1 tablespoon fish sauce
1/4 cup (60ml) lime juice
chickpea salad
2 x 300g cans chickpeas, rinsed, drained
2 medium egg tomatoes (150g), chopped coarsely
2 green onions, chopped finely
2 tablespoons lime juice
1 cup chopped fresh coriander
1 tablespoon olive oil

Cook chicken, in batches, on heated oiled
grill plate (or grill or barbecue) until almost cooked
through. Brush about two-thirds of the coriander
chilli sauce all over chicken; cook further 5 minutes
or until chicken is cooked through.
Serve chicken, sprinkled with remaining coriander
chilli sauce, with chickpea salad.
Coriander chilli sauce Blend or process
onion, garlic, chilli, coriander and sugar until
finely chopped. Add fish sauce and juice;
blend until well combined.
Chickpea salad Combine ingredients in
large bowl; toss to combine.

serves 4
per serving 16.7g fat; 1246kJ (298 cal)
on the table in 25 minutes

spaghetti with tomato and anchovy sauce

500g spaghetti
1 tablespoon olive oil
2 medium red capsicums (400g), sliced thinly
2 medium yellow capsicums (400g), sliced thinly
5 green onions, sliced thinly
2 x 415g cans tomatoes
56g can anchovy fillets, drained, chopped finely
2 tablespoons chopped fresh chives
2 tablespoons chopped fresh flat-leaf parsley

Cook pasta in large saucepan of boiling water, uncovered, until just tender; drain.
Meanwhile, heat oil in large frying pan; cook capsicums, stirring, until soft.
Add onion, undrained crushed tomatoes, anchovy and herbs; bring to a boil. Reduce heat; simmer, uncovered, about 10 minutes or until thickened slightly. Serve sauce over pasta.

serves 4
per serving 7.7g fat; 2326kJ (556 cal)
on the table in 25 minutes

veal marsala

2 tablespoons olive oil
4 veal leg steaks (500g)
1 medium brown onion (150g), chopped finely
250g button mushrooms, sliced thinly
$^1/_4$ cup (60ml) marsala
$^2/_3$ cup (160ml) beef stock
1 tablespoon chopped fresh chives

Heat oil in large frying pan. Cook veal until browned on both sides and cooked as desired; remove from pan.
Add onion to same pan; cook, stirring, until soft.
Add mushrooms, marsala and stock; stir over heat until mixture boils and thickens slightly.
Serve sauce over sliced veal; sprinkle with chives. Serve with soft instant polenta, if desired.

serves 4
per serving 11.7g fat; 1268kJ (303 cal)
on the table in 20 minutes

salad niçoise

200g small green beans
2 baby cos lettuce
4 hard-boiled eggs, quartered
425g can tuna in brine, drained, flaked
½ medium red onion (85g), sliced
200g black olives
200g cherry tomatoes, halved
dill dressing
1 tablespoon wholegrain mustard
½ cup (125ml) olive oil
⅓ cup (80ml) lemon juice
1 teaspoon bottled crushed garlic
1 tablespoon chopped fresh dill

Boil, steam or microwave beans until just tender; drain, rinse under cold water, drain.
Arrange lettuce, beans, egg, tuna, onion, olives and tomato in serving bowls; drizzle with dill dressing.
Dill dressing Combine ingredients in screw-top jar; shake well.

serves 4
per serving 38.2g fat; 2216kJ (529 cal)
on the table in 20 minutes

beef kofta with hummus

500g beef mince
1 cup (70g) stale breadcrumbs
2 teaspoons finely grated lemon rind
1 teaspoon ground cumin
1 teaspoon ground coriander
1 teaspoon bottled crushed garlic
1 egg, beaten lightly
2 medium tomatoes (380g), chopped coarsely
1 tablespoon chopped fresh flat-leaf parsley
½ cup (125g) hummus
pinch paprika

Combine beef, breadcrumbs, rind, cumin, coriander, garlic and egg in medium bowl. Divide mixture into 12 portions; roll each portion into a sausage shape, then thread onto 12 skewers.
Cook kofta in batches, on heated oiled grill plate (or grill or barbecue) until cooked through.
Meanwhile, combine tomato and parsley in medium bowl.
Serve kofta with hummus, sprinkled with paprika, and tomato mixture. Accompany with pitta bread, if desired.

serves 4
per serving 16.9g fat; 1477kJ (353 cal)
on the table in 30 minutes

chicken pho

Dried rice noodles are often labelled rice stick noodles.
You need to purchase a large barbecued chicken,
weighing approximately 900g, for this recipe.

1.5 litres (6 cups) chicken stock
2 teaspoons bottled grated ginger
1 teaspoon bottled crushed garlic
$1/4$ cup (60ml) fish sauce
1 tablespoon bottled chopped lemon grass
1 teaspoon sambal oelek
4 green onions, sliced thinly
100g dried rice noodles
4 cups (400g) shredded cooked chicken
1 cup (80g) bean sprouts
$1/2$ cup firmly packed fresh mint leaves
$1/4$ cup firmly packed fresh coriander leaves

Combine stock, ginger, garlic, sauce and
lemon grass in large saucepan; bring to a boil.
Reduce heat; simmer, covered, 8 minutes.
Remove from heat; stir in sambal oelek and onion.
Meanwhile, place noodles in medium heatproof
bowl; cover with boiling water. Stand until just
tender; drain.
Divide noodles among serving bowls; top with
chicken. Ladle soup over chicken; top with
sprouts, mint and coriander.

serves 4
per serving 2g fat; 552kJ (132 cal)
on the table in 30 minutes

fettuccine with cauliflower and broccoli

*You need half a medium cauliflower and about
450g broccoli for this recipe.*

250g fettuccine
4 cups coarsely chopped cauliflower (350g)
4 cups coarsely chopped broccoli (350g)
80g butter
3 teaspoons bottled crushed garlic
1/2 cup (35g) stale breadcrumbs
2 anchovy fillets, chopped coarsely

Cook pasta in large saucepan of boiling water,
uncovered, until just tender; drain.
Meanwhile, bring large saucepan of water to a boil.
Add cauliflower and broccoli; cook until just tender,
drain. Rinse under cold water, drain.
Heat butter in large frying pan, add garlic and
breadcrumbs; cook, stirring, until breadcrumbs
are golden brown. Stir in anchovy.
Combine pasta in large bowl with cauliflower,
broccoli and breadcrumb mixture.

serves 4
per serving 18.1g fat; 1824kJ (436 cal)
on the table in 30 minutes

lamb cutlets with white bean salad

12 lamb cutlets (800g)
2 x 300g cans white beans, rinsed, drained
3 large egg tomatoes (270g),
    seeded, chopped finely
2 lebanese cucumbers (260g), seeded,
    chopped finely
1 small red onion (100g), chopped finely
$1/4$ cup (60ml) lemon juice
1 tablespoon wholegrain mustard
$1/3$ cup (80ml) olive oil
2 tablespoons chopped fresh flat-leaf parsley

Cook lamb, in batches, on heated oiled
grill plate (or grill or barbecue) until browned
both sides and cooked as desired.
Meanwhile, combine remaining ingredients
in medium bowl.
Serve cutlets with white bean salad.

serves 4
per serving 27.9g fat; 1584kJ (378 cal)
on the table in 20 minutes

lemon pepper veal cutlets

8 veal cutlets (1kg)
1 tablespoon lemon pepper seasoning
1 teaspoon bottled crushed garlic
$^1/_4$ cup (60ml) dry white wine
$^3/_4$ cup (180ml) chicken stock
1 tablespoon lemon juice
$^1/_4$ cup chopped fresh chives

Sprinkle veal with lemon pepper. Cook veal in heated oiled non-stick frying pan until browned on both sides and cooked as desired. Remove from pan, cover to keep warm.
Add garlic and wine to same pan; bring to a boil. Add stock and juice; boil, uncovered, until reduced by half. Stir in chives. Serve sauce over veal. Serve with steamed baby potatoes, sour cream and broccolini, if desired.

serves 4
per serving 6.5g fat; 1083kJ (259 cal)
on the table in 15 minutes

thai-style pumpkin and chicken soup

¼ cup (60g) red curry paste
2 x 510g cans pumpkin soup
2 x 400ml cans coconut milk
1 cup (250ml) chicken stock
2 chicken breast fillets (340g), sliced thinly
4 green onions, sliced thinly
2 tablespoons chopped fresh coriander

Add curry paste to heated oiled medium saucepan; cook, stirring, until fragrant. Add pumpkin soup, coconut milk and stock to pan; bring to a boil.
Add chicken and stir until cooked through. Stir in onion and coriander.

serves 4
per serving 58g fat; 3206kJ (766 cal)
on the table in 15 minutes

chicken and couscous salad

²/₃ cup (160ml) chicken stock
20g butter
²/₃ cup (130g) couscous
2 teaspoons finely grated lemon rind
1 tablespoon olive oil
800g chicken tenderloins, chopped coarsely
¹/₃ cup (90g) sun-dried tomato pesto
2 tablespoons lemon juice
250g baby rocket

Bring stock to a boil in medium saucepan; stir in butter, couscous and rind. Remove from heat; stand, covered, fluffing couscous with fork occasionally, about 5 minutes or until water is absorbed.

Meanwhile, heat oil in wok or large frying pan; stir-fry chicken, in batches, until browned all over and cooked through.

Whisk pesto and juice in large bowl. Add couscous, chicken and rocket; toss gently to combine.

serves 4
per serving 29.4g fat; 2425kJ (579 cal)
on the table in 20 minutes

potato and bacon frittata

2 tablespoons olive oil
1 large brown onion (200g), halved, sliced thinly
5 bacon rashers (350g), chopped coarsely
2 teaspoons bottled crushed garlic
1kg potatoes, peeled, chopped coarsely
6 eggs
2 tablespoons water

Heat half of the oil in non-stick frying pan (base measurement 21cm, top measurement 28cm); cook onion, bacon and garlic, stirring, until onion is soft. Add potato; cook, stirring, about 10 minutes or until tender.

Transfer potato mixture to medium bowl, clean frying pan. Coat inside of pan with remaining oil. Spread potato mixture in pan.

Whisk eggs and the water in medium bowl until well combined; pour over potato mixture. Cook frittata over low heat, covered loosely with foil, about 8 minutes or until base is browned.

Place frittata under hot grill until it has set, and top is browned. Serve frittata with a mixed green salad, if desired.

serves 4
per serving 25g fat; 2049kJ (489 cal)
on the table in 40 minutes

chicken satay

The spiciness of this dish will depend on which brand of satay sauce you use.

1 tablespoon peanut oil
800g chicken tenderloins, halved
2 large brown onions (400g), sliced thickly
1 teaspoon bottled crushed garlic
$^1/_4$ cup (60ml) chicken stock
$^2/_3$ cup (160ml) coconut milk
$^3/_4$ cup (180ml) satay sauce

Heat oil in wok or large frying pan; stir-fry chicken, in batches, until browned all over and cooked through.
Place onion and garlic in same wok; stir-fry until onion softens. Return chicken to wok with remaining ingredients; stir-fry until sauce thickens slightly. Serve topped with green onion curls, if desired.

serves 4
per serving 29.2g fat; 2141kJ (511 cal)
on the table in 20 minutes

chicken tikka

2 tablespoons tikka masala paste
2 tablespoons mango chutney
1kg chicken thigh fillets, sliced thinly
$1/3$ cup (80ml) chicken stock
$1/2$ cup (140g) yogurt
$1/2$ cup chopped fresh coriander
2 teaspoons lime juice
1 fresh red thai chilli, sliced thinly

Combine paste, chutney and chicken in large bowl.
Heat wok or large frying pan; stir-fry chicken mixture,
in batches, until chicken is browned all over.
Return chicken to wok, add remaining ingredients;
bring to a boil. Reduce heat; simmer, uncovered,
about 5 minutes or until chicken is cooked through.
If desired, serve tikka with steamed basmati rice,
topped with a drizzle of yogurt and coriander leaves.

serves 4
per serving 21g fat; 1744kJ (417 cal)
on the table in 25 minutes

moroccan chickpea soup

1 tablespoon olive oil
1 large brown onion (200g), chopped finely
2 teaspoons bottled crushed garlic
1 tablespoon bottled grated ginger
1½ teaspoons ground cumin
1½ teaspoons ground coriander
1 teaspoon ground turmeric
½ teaspoon sweet paprika
¼ teaspoon ground cinnamon
1.5 litres (6 cups) vegetable stock
2 x 300g cans chickpeas, rinsed, drained
2 x 415g cans tomatoes
1 teaspoon grated lemon rind
1 tablespoon chopped fresh coriander

Heat oil in large saucepan; cook onion, garlic and ginger, stirring, until onion is soft. Add spices; cook, stirring, until fragrant.
Stir in stock, chickpeas and undrained crushed tomatoes; bring to a boil. Reduce heat; simmer, uncovered, 15 minutes or until soup thickens slightly. Just before serving, stir in rind and coriander.

serves 4
per serving 9g fat; 1018kJ (243 cal)
on the table in 25 minutes

pesto chicken salad

1/3 cup (90g) basil pesto
2 tablespoons balsamic vinegar
4 chicken breast fillets (680g)
6 medium egg tomatoes (450g), halved
125g baby rocket
1 tablespoon olive oil

Combine pesto and vinegar in small bowl;
divide mixture in two portions.
Place chicken and tomato on oven tray;
brush one portion of the pesto mixture over
chicken and tomato.
Cook tomato on heated oiled grill plate (or grill
or barbecue) until just softened; remove from plate.
Cook chicken on same grill plate until browned
both sides and cooked through. Stand 5 minutes;
slice thickly.
Place tomato and chicken in large bowl with
rocket. Add oil and remaining pesto mixture;
toss gently to combine.

serves 4
per serving 23.2g fat; 1602kJ (383 cal)
on the table in 20 minutes

wok-tossed honey soy chicken wings

12 large chicken wings (1.5kg)
2 teaspoons bottled crushed garlic
1 tablespoon bottled grated ginger
1 tablespoon peanut oil
1 tablespoon fish sauce
1 tablespoon soy sauce
¼ cup (90g) honey
2 green onions, sliced thinly

Cut wing tips from chicken; cut wings in
half at joint.

Combine chicken in large bowl with garlic
and ginger. Heat oil in wok or large frying pan;
stir-fry chicken mixture, in batches, until chicken
is lightly browned.

Return chicken mixture to wok. Add sauces
and honey; stir-fry until well coated. Cover wok;
cook, stirring occasionally, about 10 minutes
or until chicken is cooked through. Serve topped
with onion.

serves 4
per serving 40.6g fat; 2587kJ (618 cal)
on the table in 25 minutes

salmon kedgeree

You will need to cook about 1 1/3 cups (265g) rice for this recipe.

1 tablespoon olive oil
1 large brown onion (300g), sliced thinly
60g butter, chopped
1 teaspoon bottled crushed garlic
2 teaspoons curry powder
4 green onions, sliced thinly
1/3 cup (40g) frozen peas
4 cups cooked rice
415g can red salmon, drained
2 tablespoons chopped fresh flat-leaf parsley
1 tablespoon lemon juice
3 hard-boiled eggs, chopped coarsely

Heat oil in large frying pan; cook brown onion, stirring, until browned. Remove from pan; keep warm.
Heat butter in same pan; cook garlic, curry powder and green onion, stirring, until fragrant.
Add peas, rice and salmon, stir until heated through. Stir in parsley and juice. Serve kedgeree topped with eggs and brown onion.

serves 4
per serving 30.2g fat; 2594kJ (620 cal)
on the table in 20 minutes

pork with white bean puree

4 pork cutlets (1kg)
250g cherry tomatoes
2 tablespoons olive oil
2 x 300g cans white beans, rinsed, drained
2 teaspoons bottled crushed garlic
1 tablespoon lemon juice

Brush pork and tomatoes with half of the oil;
cook pork and tomatoes on heated oiled grill plate
(or grill or barbecue) until pork is browned on both
sides and cooked through, and tomatoes are soft.
Meanwhile, place beans in medium saucepan,
cover with water; bring to a boil, then simmer,
uncovered, until beans are heated through.
Drain well.
Blend or process beans with remaining oil,
garlic and juice until smooth.
Serve pork with tomatoes and white bean puree
and, if desired, lemon wedges.

serves 4
per serving 16.7g fat; 1298kJ (310 cal)
on the table in 20 minutes

mustard and rosemary chicken

You need two lemons for this recipe.

4 single chicken breast fillets (680g)
1 tablespoon wholegrain mustard
1 tablespoon lemon juice
1 tablespoon olive oil
1 tablespoon chopped fresh rosemary
1 teaspoon bottled crushed garlic
600g baby new potatoes, quartered
250g baby spinach leaves
20g butter
1 medium lemon (140g), quartered

Combine chicken, mustard, juice, oil, rosemary and garlic in medium bowl; toss to coat chicken in mustard mixture.
Cook chicken, in batches, on heated oiled grill plate (or grill or barbecue) until chicken is browned both sides and cooked through.
Meanwhile, boil, steam or microwave potato until just tender; drain. Place hot potato in large bowl with spinach and butter; toss gently until butter melts and spinach just wilts.
Serve chicken with vegetables and lemon.

serves 4
per serving 18.5g fat; 1785kJ (426 cal)
on the table in 20 minutes

bucatini with moroccan lamb sauce

375g bucatini pasta
2 teaspoons olive oil
1 small brown onion (80g), chopped finely
1 teaspoon bottled crushed garlic
500g lamb mince
1 teaspoon ground cumin
$1/2$ teaspoon cayenne pepper
$1/2$ teaspoon ground cinnamon
2 tablespoons tomato paste
2 x 415g cans tomatoes
1 large zucchini (150g), chopped coarsely
2 tablespoons chopped fresh mint

Cook pasta in large saucepan of boiling water, uncovered, until just tender; drain.
Meanwhile, heat oil in large saucepan, add onion and garlic; cook, stirring, until onion is soft. Add lamb; cook, stirring, until lamb changes colour. Add spices; cook, stirring, until fragrant.
Stir in tomato paste, undrained crushed tomatoes and zucchini; bring to a boil. Reduce heat; simmer, uncovered, about 15 minutes or until sauce thickens slightly. Stir in mint.
Serve pasta topped with sauce.

serves 4
per serving 16.3g fat; 2527kJ (604 cal)
on the table in 30 minutes

warm lamb, potato and pesto salad

600g baby new potatoes, chopped
1 tablespoon olive oil
8 lamb fillets (600g)
280g jar char-grilled eggplant, drained, chopped
200g baby spinach leaves
8 fresh basil leaves
$1/3$ cup (80g) bottled char-grilled vegetable pesto
1 tablespoon lemon juice

Boil, steam or microwave potato until tender; drain.
Meanwhile, heat oil in large frying pan, cook lamb
until browned all over and cooked as desired.
Stand lamb about 2 minutes before slicing thickly.
Place warm potato and lamb in large bowl
with remaining ingredients; toss gently.

serves 4
per serving 26.1g fat; 2166kJ (517 cal)
on the table in 15 minutes

glossary

bacon rashers also known as slices of bacon, made from pork side, cured and smoked.

balsamic vinegar authentic only from the province of Modena, Italy; made from a regional wine of white Trebbiano grapes aged in antique wooden casks to give the exquisite pungent flavour.

bean sprouts also known as bean shoots; tender new growths of assorted beans and seeds germinated for consumption as sprouts.

black bean sauce a Chinese sauce made from fermented soy beans, spices, water and wheat flour.

breadcrumbs, stale one- or two-day-old bread made into crumbs by grating, blending or processing.

butter use salted or unsalted (sweet) butter; 125g is equal to one stick of butter.

capsicum also known as bell pepper or, simply, pepper. Seeds and membranes should be discarded before use; available in several colours, each of which has an individual flavour.

cayenne pepper a thin-fleshed, long, extremely hot red chilli; usually purchased dried and ground.

cheese

cheddar: a semi-hard cow-milk cheese. It ranges in colour from white to pale-yellow and has a slightly crumbly texture if properly matured. It's aged for between nine months and two years and the flavour becomes sharper with time.

fetta: a white cheese with milky, fresh acidity; one of the cornerstones of Turkish, Greek and Bulgarian cooking. Today it is most commonly made from cow milk, though sheep- and goat-milk varieties are available. Fetta is solid but crumbles readily.

pizza: a commercial blend of varying proportions of processed grated mozzarella, cheddar and parmesan.

chicken

breast fillet: skinned, boned chicken breast.

tenderloins: thin strip of meat lying just under the breast.

thigh fillets: skinned and boned thigh.

chickpeas also called garbanzos, hummus or channa; an irregularly round, sandy-coloured legume used extensively in Mediterranean and Latin cooking.

chilli

bottled: conveniently bottled chopped chillies.

dried flakes: dehydrated extremely fine slices and whole seeds; good for cooking or for sprinkling over cooked food.

thai: small hot chilli; bright-red to dark-green in colour.

chives related to the onion and leek; possess subtle onion flavour.

coconut milk second pressing from grated mature coconut flesh; available in cans and cartons.

coriander also known as pak chee, cilantro or chinese parsley; bright-green leafy herb with a pungent flavour.

cornflour also known as cornstarch; used as a thickening agent in cooking.

couscous a fine, grain-like cereal product, originally from North Africa; made from semolina.

cumin, ground also known as zeera.

eggs some recipes in this book may call for raw or barely cooked eggs; exercise caution if there is a salmonella problem in your area.

fish sauce called nam pla on the label if it is Thai made; the Vietnamese version, nuoc nam, is almost identical. Made from pulverised salted fermented fish (most often anchovies); has a pungent smell and strong taste.

flat-leaf parsley also known as continental or italian parsley.

garlic, bottled conveniently bottled crushed garlic.

ginger, bottled conveniently bottled grated ginger.

hummus a Middle-Eastern salad or dip made from softened dried chickpeas, garlic, lemon juice and tahini (sesame seed paste); can be purchased, ready-made, from most delicatessens and supermarkets.

lamb cutlets small, tender rib chop.

lebanese cucumber long, slender and thin-skinned; this variety also known as the european or burpless cucumber.

lemon grass, bottled conveniently bottled chopped lemon grass.

lemon pepper seasoning
a blend of crushed black
pepper, lemon, herbs
and spices.

marsala a sweet fortified
wine, originally from Sicily.

mince ground meat.

mushrooms

button: small, cultivated white
mushrooms with mild flavour.

flat: large, flat mushrooms with
a rich earthy flavour. They are
sometimes misnamed field
mushrooms which are
wild mushrooms.

mustard, wholegrain also
known as seeded. A French-
style coarse-grain mustard
made from crushed mustard
seeds and dijon-style
French mustard.

noodles

dried rice: dried noodles
made from rice flour and
water, available flat and wide
or very thin (vermicelli). Should
be soaked in boiling water
to soften. Also known as
rice stick noodles.

dried wheat: extremely
thin dried noodle made
from wheat flour.

oil

olive: made from ripened
olives. Extra virgin and virgin
are the best while extra light
or light refers to taste not
fat levels.

peanut: pressed from ground
peanuts; most commonly
used oil in Asian cooking
because of its high smoke
point (capacity to handle high
heat without burning).

sesame: made from roasted,
crushed, white sesame
seeds; a flavouring rather
than a cooking medium.

onion

green: also known as scallion
or (incorrectly) shallot; an
immature onion picked before
the bulb has formed, having a
long, bright-green edible stalk.

red: also known as spanish,
red spanish or bermuda
onion; a sweet-flavoured,
large, purple-red onion.

spring: have crisp, narrow,
green-leafed tops and a
large, sweet white bulb.

oyster sauce Asian in origin,
this rich, brown sauce is
made from oysters and their
brine, salt and soy sauce, and
thickened with starches.

paprika ground dried red
capsicum (bell pepper),
available sweet or hot.

red curry paste commercially
packaged curry paste; made
with red chilli, onion, garlic, oil,
lemon, shrimp paste, cumin,
paprika, turmeric and pepper.

rocket also known as arugula,
rugula and rucola; a peppery-
tasting green leaf which can
be eaten raw in salad or
used in cooking.

**sambal oelek (also ulek or
olek)** Indonesian in origin; a
salty paste made from ground
chillies and vinegar.

satay sauce traditional
Indonesian/Malaysian spicy
peanut sauce. Make your
own or buy one of the
many packaged versions
easily obtained from
supermarkets or specialty
Asian food stores.

snow peas also called
mange tout ("eat all"). Snow
pea tendrils, the growing
shoots of the plant, are sold
by green grocers.

soy sauce also known as
sieu; made from fermented
soy beans. Several variations
are available.

spinach also known
as english spinach and,
incorrectly, silverbeet.
Tender green leaves are good
raw in salads or added to
soups, stir-fries and stews.

stock 1 cup (250ml) stock
is the equivalent of 1 cup
(250ml) water plus 1 crumbled
stock cube (or 1 teaspoon
stock powder).

sugar we used coarse,
granulated table sugar, also
known as crystal sugar,
unless otherwise specified.

brown: an extremely soft, fine
granulated sugar retaining
molasses for its characteristic
colour and flavour.

caster: also known as
superfine or finely granulated
table sugar.

tikka masala paste consists
of chilli, coriander, cumin, lentil
flour, garlic, ginger, oil, fennel,
turmeric, pepper, cloves,
cinnamon and cardamom.

tomato

egg: also called plum or
roma, these are smallish,
oval-shaped tomatoes.

paste: triple-concentrated
tomato puree used to flavour
soups, stews and sauces.

white beans, canned often
labelled as butter beans but
are, in fact, cannellini beans.
A large beige bean having a
mealy texture and mild taste.

yogurt we used plain,
unflavoured yogurt, unless
otherwise specified.

zucchini also known
as courgette.

index

facts & figures

These conversions are approximate only, but the difference between an exact and the approximate conversion of various liquid and dry measures is minimal and will not affect your cooking results.

Note: NZ, Canada, US and UK all use 15ml tablespoons. Australian tablespoons measure 20ml. All cup and spoon measurements are level.

Measuring equipment

The difference between one country's measuring cups and another's is, at most, within a 2 or 3 teaspoon variance. (For the record, 1 Australian metric measuring cup holds approximately 250ml.) The most accurate way of measuring dry ingredients is to weigh them. For liquids, use a clear glass or plastic jug having metric markings.

How to measure

When using graduated measuring cups, shake dry ingredients loosely into the appropriate cup. Do not tap the cup on a bench or tightly pack the ingredients unless directed to do so. Level the top of measuring cups and measuring spoons with a knife. When measuring liquids, place a clear glass or plastic jug having metric markings on a flat surface to check accuracy at eye level.

Dry measures

metric	imperial
15g	½oz
30g	1oz
60g	2oz
90g	3oz
125g	4oz (¼lb)
155g	5oz
185g	6oz
220g	7oz
250g	8oz (½lb)
280g	9oz
315g	10oz
345g	11oz
375g	12oz (¾lb)
410g	13oz
440g	14oz
470g	15oz
500g	16oz (1lb)
750g	24oz (1½lb)
1kg	32oz (2lb)

We use large eggs with an average weight of 60g.

Liquid measures

metric	imperial
30 ml	1 fluid oz
60 ml	2 fluid oz
100 ml	3 fluid oz
125 ml	4 fluid oz
150 ml	5 fluid oz (¼ pint/1 gill)
190 ml	6 fluid oz
250 ml (1cup)	8 fluid oz
300 ml	10 fluid oz (½ pint)
500 ml	16 fluid oz
600 ml	20 fluid oz (1 pint)
1000 ml (1litre)	1¾ pints

Helpful measures

metric	imperial
3mm	⅛in
6mm	¼in
1cm	½in
2cm	¾in
2.5cm	1in
6cm	2½in
8cm	3in
20cm	8in
23cm	9in
25cm	10in
30cm	12in (1ft)

Oven temperatures

These oven temperatures are only a guide for conventional ovens. For fan-forced ovens, check the manufacturer's manual.

	°C (Celsius)	°F (Fahrenheit)	Gas Mark
Very slow	120	250	½
Slow	150	275 – 300	1 – 2
Moderately slow	160	325	3
Moderate	180	350 – 375	4 – 5
Moderately hot	200	400	6
Hot	220	425 – 450	7 – 8
Very hot	240	475	9

ARE YOU MISSING SOME OF THE WORLD'S FAVOURITE COOKBOOKS?

The Australian Women's Weekly cookbooks are available from bookshops, cookshops, supermarkets and other stores all over the world. You can also buy direct from the publisher, using the order form below.

Mini Series £2.50 190x138mm 64 pages			
	QTY		QTY
4 Fast Ingredients		Italian	
15-minute Feasts		Jams & Jellies	
30-minute Meals		Kids Party Food	
50 Fast Chicken Fillets		Last-minute Meals	
After-work Stir-fries		Lebanese Cooking	
Barbecue		Malaysian Favourites	
Barbecue Chicken		Microwave	
Barbecued Seafood		Mince	
Biscuits, Brownies & Biscotti		Muffins	
Bites		Noodles	
Bowl Food		Party Food	
Burgers, Rösti & Fritters		Pasta	
Cafe Cakes		Pickles and Chutneys	
Cafe Food		Potatoes	
Casseroles		Risotto	
Char-grills & Barbecues		Roast	
Cheesecakes, Pavlovas & Trifles		Salads	
Chocolate		Seafood	
Chocolate Cakes		Simple Slices	
Christmas Cakes & Puddings		Simply Seafood	
Cocktails		Skinny Food	
Curries		Stir-fries	
Drinks		Summer Salads	
Fast Fish		Tapas, Antipasto & Mezze	
Fast Food for Friends		Thai Cooking	
Fast Soup		Thai Favourites	
Finger Food		Vegetarian	
From the Shelf		Vegetarian Stir-fries	
Gluten-free Cooking		Vegie Main Meals	
Ice-creams & Sorbets		Wok	
Indian Cooking		**TOTAL COST**	**£**

NAME

ADDRESS

POSTCODE

DAYTIME PHONE

I ENCLOSE MY CHEQUE/MONEY ORDER FOR £

OR PLEASE CHARGE MY VISA, ACCESS OR MASTERCARD NUMBER

CARDHOLDER'S NAME

EXPIRY DATE

CARDHOLDER'S SIGNATURE

To order: Mail or fax – photocopy or complete the order form above, and send your credit card details or cheque payable to: Australian Consolidated Press (UK), Moulton Park Business Centre, Red House Road, Moulton Park, Northampton NN6 4AQ, phone (+44) (01) 604 497531, fax (+44) (01) 604 497533, e-mail books@acpuk.com. Or order online at **www.acpuk.com**
Non-UK residents: We accept the credit cards listed on the coupon, or cheques, drafts or International Money Orders payable in sterling and drawn on a UK bank. Credit card charges are at the exchange rate current at the time of payment.
Postage and packing UK: Add £1.00 per order plus 25p per book.
Postage and packing overseas: Add £2.00 per order plus 50p per book.
Offer ends 31.12.2006

Food director Pamela Clark
Food editor Louise Patniotis
ACP BOOKS
Editorial director Susan Tomnay
Creative director Hieu Chi Nguyen
Senior editor Julie Collard
Designer Mary Keep
Sales director Brian Ceames
Brand manager Renée Crea
Production manager Carol Currie
Chief executive officer John Alexander
Group publisher Pat Ingram
Publisher Sue Wannan
Editorial director (AWW) Deborah Thomas

Produced by ACP Books, Sydney.
Printing by Dai Nippon Printing in Korea.
Published by ACP Publishing Pty Limited,
54 Park St, Sydney;
GPO Box 4088, Sydney, NSW 2001.
Ph: (02) 9282 8618 Fax: (02) 9267 9438.
acpbooks@acp.com.au
www.acpbooks.com.au
To order books phone 136 116.
Send recipe enquiries to
Recipeenquiries@acp.com.au
RIGHTS ENQUIRIES
Laura Bamford, Director ACP Books.
lbamford@acplon.co.uk
Ph: +44 (207) 812 6526
Australia Distributed by Network Services,
GPO Box 4088, Sydney, NSW 1028.
Ph: (02) 9282 8777 Fax: (02) 9264 3278.
United Kingdom Distributed by Australian
Consolidated Press (UK), Moulton Park Busine
Centre, Red House Road, Moulton Park,
Northampton, NN3 6AQ. Ph: (01604) 497 531
Fax: (01604) 497 533 acpukltd@aol.com
Canada Distributed by Whitecap Books Ltd,
351 Lynn Ave, North Vancouver, BC, V7J 2C4
Ph: (604) 980 9852 Fax: (604) 980 8197
customerservice@whitecap.ca
www.whitecap.ca
New Zealand Distributed by Netlink Distributic
Company, ACP Media Centre, Cnr Fanshawe
and Beaumont Streets, Westhaven, Auckland.
PO Box 47906, Ponsonby, Auckland, NZ.
Ph: (9) 366 9966 ask@ndc.co.nz
South Africa Distributed by PSD Promotions,
30 Diesel Road, Isando, Gauteng, Johannesb
PO Box 1175, Isando, 1600, Gauteng, Johanne
Ph: (27 11) 392 6065/6/7 Fax: (27 11) 392 60
orders@psdprom.co.za

Clark, Pamela.
The Australian Women's Weekly
Last-minute Meals.

Includes index.
ISBN 1 86396 304 9

1. Quick and easy cookery.
I. Title. II. Title: Last-minute Meals.
III. Title: Australian Women's Weekly.

641.555
© ACP Magazines Ltd 2003
ABN 18 053 273 546

This publication is copyright. No part of it may
reproduced or transmitted in any form without
written permission of the publishers.

First published 2003. Reprinted 2005.

Cover Spicy orange lamb noodle stir-fry, pag
Stylist Hieu Chi Nguyen
Photographer Ian Wallace
Home economist Kelly Cruickshanks
Back cover at left, Chilli and honey beef, pag
at right, Salad niçoise, page 22.